Marx

Capital

Essential extracts

(Basic economics for bankers)

Charles Allcock

©

Published in 2010 by

Thurlwood Numerical Devices ltd

Park Nook Farm, Ipstones, Stoke-on-Trent,

Staffordshire. St10 2ng

www.thurlwoodnumerical.co.uk

© Charles Allcock

ISBN   978-0-9566079-0-4

Contents

Book 1

A critical analysis of capitalist production

Book 2

The process of circulation of capital

Preface

Years ago I bought a copy of Karl Marx's Capital and was surprised by its contents. Why should this be? Its title told me it was all about economics and how the capitalist system functions. I thought it would be a book about socialism. But it is not. Luckily I read it. I knew absolutely nothing about economics and found it hard to read at first, but as I got into it, I found it made a lot of sense. The analysis is thorough and convincing. I found it similar to a body of mathematics in its structure and rigour, like the primitive terms in geometry that are used to build into axioms and theorems that describe three dimensional physical space Marx does something similar for the social economic space.

Many are put off reading it because they also believe it to be about socialism (or communism) and some consider it to be politically correct to make a point of not having read it. It often receives adverse criticism in the media by commentators and politicians who have probably not even read it. One reason for this could be the bad behaviour of some that call themselves "Marxists" (who've probably not read it either). This prejudice preventing it from being read is a great loss to free market capitalism, so I have tried to put the ideas contained in volumes one and two into a reduced form, by taking relevant extracts that are able to convey the general contents. By making it easier and quicker to read, more may know the "true" Karl Marx Capital. And of course its sheer size (it could be used as a door stop) could put off the most well intentioned attempts to read it.

BOOK 1

A critical analysis

of

Capitalist Production

Commodities

The wealth of those societies in which the capitalist mode of production prevails, presents itself as an immense accumulation of commodities, its unit being a single commodity. Our investigation must therefore begin with the analysis of a commodity.

Commodities are every day items that have a use-value, such as a loaf of bread, a coat or a pair of shoes. Cars, houses, aeroplanes, coal and oil, are also commodities, and these constitute the wealth in a capitalist society. Each has its own particular use-value. Commodities also have exchange value and in the past they were exchanged for each other in various relative amounts.

$$x \text{ amount of corn} = y \text{ amount of cloth}$$

For different items to be equal to each other they must contain something that is equal. What all commodities contain in common is human labour, and it is the amount of labour contained in them that is being equated. Commodities are deposits of homogeneous human labour. The amount of labour must be the amount that is socially necessary using average skill and intensity. Their value can only be expressed by being exchanged with one another.

As the productivity of labour increases the value of commodities falls, and visa versa. A use-value only has value if labour is expended on it. A use-value with value is not a commodity unless it is exchanged for other commodities. Nothing can have value without having use-value.

Commodities can only stand in relation to each other because the labour that produces them is of different types or trades. The division of labour is a necessary condition for the production of commodities.

The production of commodities implies the division of labour.

Useful labour is a necessary condition for the existence of the human race. Existence of the human race implies expenditure of useful labour.

A commodity may be the product of the most

skilled labour, but its value by equating it to the product of simple unskilled labour, represents a definite quantity of the latter labour alone.

An increase in the quantity of use-values is an increase of material wealth. With two coats two men can be clothed, but an increased quantity of material wealth may correspond to a simultaneous fall in the magnitude of value. With increased productivity more products are created for a given amount of labour. The labour in each will be less, so will its value, and visa versa.

The elementary form of value

A product becomes a commodity when the labour spent on the production of a useful article and therefore giving it value becomes the primary objective.

E.g.   20 metres of linen   =   1 coat

A use-value can only express its value in terms of some other use-value. The dominant relationship

3

between man and man is that of owners of commodities.

Expanded form of value

E.g.   20 metres of linen = 1 coat = 5 kilos of tea = 20 kilos of coffee = 30 kilos of corn = 1 ounce of gold = 500 kilos of iron

Every other commodity becomes a mirror of the linens value, showing that they all contain undifferentiated human labour and this determines their exchange proportions.

General form of value

E.g.

1 coat

5 kilos of tea

20 kilos of coffee

30 kilos of corn   =   20 metres of linen

1 ounce of gold

500 kilos of iron

Etc.

The elementary form of value occurs practically only at the beginning, when products of labour are converted into commodities by accidental and occasional exchanges. The expanded form of value occurs when a particular product of labour such as cattle is no longer exceptionally, but habitually exchanged for various other commodities. The general form of value occurs when a commodity acquires a general expression of its value by all other commodities simultaneously. The commodity that becomes the universal equivalent now becomes the money commodity or serves as money. Gold in particular has attained this role.

The money form

E.g.   20 metres of linen
        1 coat
        20 kilos of coffee   =   1 ounce of gold
        30 kilos of corn
        500 kilos of iron
        X commodity A

The relative value of linen in price-form is :-

20 metres of linen = 1 ounce of gold.

The fetishism of commodities

The division of a product into a useful thing and a value becomes practically important only when exchange has acquired a level at which useful articles are produced for the purpose of being exchanged, and their character as values has to be taken into account. Labour must now:

1.   Satisfy a definite social need and be part of the collective labour of all.

2.   Satisfy the manifold needs of the producer by exchange.

The social character of labour requires that products must not only be useful, but useful to others and the different types of labour are socially equal by having value.

In more primitive organisations the social character of labour is not reflected through commodities and can be seen directly. E.g. peasant family or feudal village. The establishment of commodities in these older communities coincide with their dissolution.

Spontaneously developed branches of the social division of labour, are continually being reduced to the quantitative proportions in which society requires them. And why? Because, in the midst of all the accidental and ever fluctuating exchange-relations between the products, the labour-time socially necessary for their production forcibly asserts itself like an over-riding law of nature.

Exchange

Exchange must take place before a commodity can realise its use-value. Commodities must be realised as values before they can be realised as use-values. The need for a universal equivalent to facilitate exchange develops one special commodity into money. Because early societies were based on

7

property in common, exchange begins on the boundaries of such communities. But once begun alienation spreads within the community. The universal equivalent or money-form first attaches itself to the most important articles of exchange from outside or objects that form the main portion of wealth, i.e. cattle. Nomads were probably the first to use the money form.

Gold and silver of uniform quality is divisible and reunite-able. Gold and silver are still commodities. The value of money is expressed by the quantity of any other commodity that costs the same amount of labour time. This takes place at the source of production when its steps into circulation by means of barter. Once gold is established as money, every commodity has its value expressed in it, because it is money. Gold as a standard of price means relating exchange to a quantity of gold. Used as a standard of value means relating exchange to the value of the gold.

Commodity prices can rise if their values rise, the

value of money remaining constant, or from a fall in the value of money, the value of the commodities remaining constant and visa versa. A quarter ounce of gold becomes a pound which is divided into shillings[2] and pennies the legally valid names of the subdivisions of the gold standard. Money can serve as *money of account* when used as a method of valuing an article in money-form.

The circulation of commodities

A producer of a particular type of commodity must first sell his own, and convert its value into money before he can buy the commodities that he wishes to purchase for himself. That is the act of selling in order to buy.

20yds of linen	$\rightarrow$	money £2	$\rightarrow$	1 bible
C	$\rightarrow$	M	$\rightarrow$	C

---

[2] Pre-decimalization there were 12 pennies in 1 shilling, and 20 shillings in 1£.

The result is C → C the exchange of one commodity for another. This is the circulation of materialised social labour. Labour must be socially useful, i.e. of a branch of the social division of labour. This is changing as new products are brought out or as others are no longer wanted. The market must not be saturated and can be above or below value. Ones own labour is alienated so as to appropriate produce of others' labour. When they assume the money shape, commodities strip off every trace of their natural use-value and of their particular kind of labour to which they owe their creation, in order to transform themselves into uniform socially recognised incarnation of homogeneous human labour.

Money does not vanish after a commodity has been exchanged but reappears in the place vacated by another commodity. If the split between the sale and purchase becomes too pronounced, the intimate connexion between them, their oneness, asserts itself by producing a crisis.

The medium of circulation keeps continually

within the sphere of circulation and moves about in it, but commodities move in, then out. How much money does this sphere constantly absorb?

Amount in circulation = total of prices of exchange commodities.

If the value of gold rises or falls, the sum of the prices of commodities fall or rise, and the quantity of money in currency must fall or rise to the same extent. The value of precious metals at the point of production will percolate through the system. The quantity of circulating money varies with prices of commodities, 4 articles of £2 each at different localities needs £8 to circulate, but 4 articles in succession, A → £2 → B → £2 → C → £2 → D → £2 , needs only £2.

The velocity of currency of money is measured by the number of moves made by a given piece of money in a given time. The quantity of money functioning as a circulating medium is equal to the sum of the prices

11

of commodities divided by the number of moves made by coins of the same denomination. Since the amount of money capable of being absorbed by the circulation is calculate-able for a given mean velocity of currency, all that is necessary in order to abstract a number of sovereigns from circulation is to throw the same number of bank notes into it, a device well known to all bankers.

Due to the wear and loss of metal from coins, they can become a symbol of the weight they should officially contain. This implies the latent possibility of replacing metallic coins by tokens of some other material, e.g. paper.

The issue of paper money only represents the amount of gold (or silver) required for the circulation of commodities. If more is put into circulation it still only represents the amount of gold required. To double the amount of paper would double prices. Only in so far as paper money represents gold, which like all other commodities has value, is it a symbol of value.

Money

The commodity that functions as a measure of value and either in its own person or by a representative as a medium of circulation, is money.

As money removes the qualitative differences of commodities it does away with all distinctions. But money is a commodity and so can become private property of any individual. Thus social power becomes private power of private persons. Money has no bounds to its efficacy, qualitatively, but has quantitatively to each sum of money.

To make a hoard, money must be prevented from circulating. Hard work, saving, and avarice are therefore the hoarders three cardinal virtues, and to sell much and buy little is the sum of his political economy. Due to changes in amount and time for the circulation of commodities and price changes, the quantity of money needed to circulate them continually changes. In order that the mass of money actually current may constantly saturate the absorbing power of circulation it is necessary that the quantity of gold and silver in a country be greater than the quantity required to function as coin. This condition is fulfilled by money taking the form of hoards.

Because of timing in production and distribution, vendor and purchaser cannot be matched immediately. The vendor becomes a creditor, the purchaser becomes a debtor and money becomes the "means of payment". These new roles can be just as transient and alternating as those of seller and buyer, and in turns played by the same actors.

Money acts as a measure of value and a means of payment. The contract price measures the obligation of the debtor. At the end of the contract period the circulating medium comes into circulation leaving the hands of the buyer for that of the seller. The circulating medium between times has been in the form of a hoard. The means of payment enters circulation but only after the commodity has left it.

The fact that a number of sales take

place simultaneously, and side by side, limits the extent to which coin can be replaced by the rapidity of currency. However in proportion as payments are concentrated at one spot, special institutions and methods are developed for their liquidation, ie by their balancing out. The greater the amount of payments concentrated, the less is the balancing payment relatively to that amount, and the less is the mass of means of payment in circulation. With money functioning only ideally as money of account and the ever lengthening chain of payments, crisis does occur. During a monetary crisis only hard cash will suffice. With increasing use of money of account and use of credit, even when prices, rapidity of currency and the extent of the economy in payments are given, the quantity of money current and the mass of commodities circulating during a given period, such as a day, no longer correspond.

Credit-money springs directly out of the function of money as a means of payment. Certificates of debt owing for the purchased commodities circulate for the purpose of transferring those debts to others. Money also begins to serve as the means of payment beyond the sphere of circulation of commodities. Rents, taxes, and such like payments are transformed from payments in kind into money payments. This makes it necessary to accumulate money against the dates fixed for the payment of the sums owing. Money especially gold and silver becomes the universal medium of payment in periods when the customary equilibrium in the exchange of products between different nations is suddenly disturbed.

Transformation of money into capital

Capital, as opposed to landed property, invariably takes the form of money at first. The circuit of capital is $M \rightarrow C \rightarrow M'$ where the aim is to increase M to $M + m = M'$, where as in $C \rightarrow M \rightarrow C$ equal values change hands for different products. The small m is surplus-value.

The aim of $C \rightarrow M \rightarrow C$ is that of consumption, it starts with one commodity, and finishes with another, which falls out of circulation and into consumption. The circulation of money as capital is an end in itself, for the expansion of value takes place only with this constantly renewed movement.

Capital is money. Capital is commodities.

Capital tries to repeat its cycle without limit. Merchant's capital, buying in order to sell dearer $M \rightarrow C \rightarrow M'$, Industrial capital is money. Interest bearing capital $M \rightarrow M'$, is the abridged version of $M \rightarrow C \rightarrow M'$.

In its normal form, the circulation of commodities demands the exchange of equivalents. The surplus-value can only come from the commodity being labour.

The owner of labour power and owner of money meet in the market and deal with each other as on the basis of equal rights, with this difference alone. That one is a buyer and the other a seller. Both equal in the eyes of the law.

In order to remain a free person the labour-

17

power must only be sold for a definite period of time. The free labourer is free in a double sense. As a free man he can dispose of his labour-power as his own commodity, and he has no other commodity for sale, and is short of everything necessary for the realisation of his labour-power.

Capital springs to life only when the owner of the means of production and subsistence meets in the market with the free labourer selling his labour-power. The value of labour power is determined by the labour time necessary for its production and reproduction, i.e. for the production of the means of subsistence.

Rate of surplus value

The value of the means of production used in the process are preserved and present themselves afresh as constituent parts of the value of the product. The values of the cotton and the spindle for instance, re-appear again in the value of the yarn. The value of the means of production is therefore preserved by being transferred to the product. The labourer also adds fresh value to the subject of his labour by expending upon it a given amount of additional labour.

The labour process may continue beyond the time necessary to re-produce and incorporate in the product the equivalent for the value of the labour-power. The action of labour-power, therefore, not only produces its own value, but produces value over and above it. This surplus-value is the difference between the value of the product and the value of the elements consumed in the formation of that product, in other words, of the means of production and the labour-power.

That part of the capital represented by the raw material, auxiliary material and instruments of labour, does not, in the process of production, undergo any quantitative alteration of value. This is therefore called constant-capital. The labour-power reproduces the equivalent of its own value, and also produces an excess, a surplus-value. This part of capital is therefore called variable capital.

Capital advanced $C = c + v$

c = constant capital

v = variable capital

When the process of production is finished, we get a commodity.

$$C' = c + v + s \qquad s = \text{surplus value}$$

The ratio of surplus-value to variable capital s/v is called "the rate of surplus-value".

The portion of the day's labour in which the labourer produces the value of his labour-power, we call "necessary" labour time. Necessary for the labourer, independently of the particular social form of his labour. Necessary as regards capital, because it's existence depends on the existence of the labourer. Labour in excess of necessary labour is surplus-labour. The quality of labour transfers the value of constant capital into the product, and the quantity of labour adds to the value to reproduce variable capital and produce surplus-value. Capitalism has not invented surplus-labour. Wherever a part of society possesses the monopoly of the means of production, the labourer, free or not free, must add to the working-time necessary for his own maintenance an extra working-time in order to produce the means of subsistence for the owners of the means of production.

An increase in the productiveness of the labourers' means of subsistence will cause a fall in the value of labour-power, by reducing the necessary labour-time. If the length of the working-day remains the same, the surplus-labour will increase and therefore the surplus-value will increase.

Surplus-value produced by the prolonging of the working-day, is called *absolute surplus-value*. The surplus-value arising from the curtailment of the necessary labour-time, and from the corresponding alteration in the respective lengths of the two components of the working-day, is called *relative surplus-value*.

If a capitalist increases productivity by a new method of production the law of determination of value by labour-time, compels him to sell his goods under their social value. This same law, acting as a coercive law of competition, forces his competitors to adopt the new method.

Hence there is immanent in capital an inclination and constant tendency to heighten the productiveness of labour in order to cheapen commodities, and by such cheapening to cheapen the labourer himself.

As the use of machinery becomes more general in a particular industry, the social value of the product sinks down to its individual value, and the law that surplus-value does not arise from labour-power that has been replaced by the machinery, but from the labour-power actually employed in working with the machinery, asserts itself. However much the use of machinery may increase the surplus-value at the expense of necessary labour by heightening productiveness of labour, it is clear that it attains this result, only by diminishing the number of workmen employed by a given amount of capital. It converts what was formerly variable capital, invested in labour-power, into machinery, which, being constant capital, does not produce surplus-value.

This contradiction comes to light, as soon as, by the general employment of machinery in a given industry, the value of the machine-produced commodity regulates the value of all commodities of the same sort. It is this contradiction, that in its turn, drives the capitalist, without his being conscious of the fact, to excessive lengthening of the working-day, in order that he may compensate the decrease in the relative number of labourers, by an increase not only of relative, but of the absolute surplus-labour. By setting free the labourers it supplants, a surplus working population, which is compelled to submit to the dictation of capital, is formed.

Where labour is repeated day after day with unvarying uniformity, a point must inevitably be reached, where extension of the working-day and the intensity of labour mutually exclude one another, in such a way that the lengthening of the working-day becomes compatible only with a lower degree of intensity, and a higher degree of intensity only with a shortening of the working-day. Increasing intensity enables more to be produced in a given time with the same expenditure of labour. Labour-time continues to transmit as before the same value to the total product, but this unchanged amount of exchange-value is spread over more use-values, hence the value of each commodity sinks. The enormous power, inherent in the factory system, of expanding by jumps, and the dependence of that system on the markets of the world, necessarily begets feverish production, followed by over-filling of the markets, whereupon contraction of the markets brings on crippling of production. The life of modern industry becomes a series of cycles of moderate activity, prosperity, over-production, crisis and stagnation.

It is only after men have raised themselves above the rank of animals, when therefore their labour has been to some extent socialised, that a condition arises in which the surplus-value of the one becomes a condition of existence of the other. At the early period, the portion of society that lives on the labour of others is infinitely small compared with the mass of direct producers. Along with progress in the productiveness of labour, that small portion of society increases both absolutely and relatively.

Accumulation of capital

The conversion of a sum of money into means of production and labour-power is the first step taken by the quantum of value that is going to function as capital. This conversion takes place in the market, within the sphere of circulation. The second step, the process of production, is complete as soon as the means of production have been converted into commodities whose value exceeds that of their component parts, and therefore, contains the capital advanced, plus a surplus-value. These must then be thrown into circulation. They must be sold, their value realised in money, this money afresh converted into capital, and so on over and over again. This circular movement, in which the same phases continually occur in succession, forms the circulation of capital.

The conditions of production are also those of reproduction. This means that part of the products are means of production, or elements of fresh products. The means of production must be replaced, i.e. the instruments of labour, the raw material, and auxiliary material consumed in the course of a year, by an equal quantity of the same kind. Hence a definite portion of each years product are for productive consumption from the very first. This portion exists, for the most part, in the shape of articles totally UN-fitted for individual consumption.

The capitalist class is constantly giving the labouring class order-notes, in the form of money, on a portion of the commodities produced by the later and appropriated by the former. The labourers give these order-notes back just as constantly to the capitalist class, and in this way get their share of their own product.

Conversion of surplus-value into capital

To accumulate it is necessary to convert a portion of the surplus-product into capital. Consequently, a part of the annual surplus-labour must have been applied to the production of additional means of production and subsistence, over and above the quantity required to replace the capital advanced. In one word, surplus-value is converted into capital solely because the surplus-product, whose value it is, already comprises the material elements of new capital.

A prejudice confuses capitalist production with hoarding, and fancies that accumulated wealth is either wealth that is rescued from being destroyed in its existing form, i.e. from being consumed, or wealth that is withdrawn from circulation. There can be no greater error than supposing that capital is increased by non-consumption. The accumulation of commodities in great masses is the result either of over-production or of a stoppage of circulation.

For personified capital, it is not values in use and the enjoyment of them, but exchange-value and its augmentation, that spur him into action.

Fanatically bent on making value expand itself, he ruthlessly forces the human race to produce for the sake of production. He thus forces the development of the productive powers of society and creates those material conditions which alone can form the real basis of a higher form of society. A society in which the full and free development of every individual forms the ruling principles. Moreover, the development of capitalist production makes it constantly necessary to keep increasing the amount of the capital laid out in a given industrial undertaking, and competition makes the immanent laws of capitalist production to be felt by each capitalist, as external coercive laws. It compels him to keep constantly extending his capital, in order to preserve it, but extend it he cannot, except by means of progressive accumulation.

The growth of capital involves the growth of its variable constituent or the part invested in labour-power. The reproduction of labour-power forms an essential of the reproduction of capital itself. Accumulation of capital is therefore an increase of the proletariat. A part of the surplus-value turned into additional capital must always be re-transformed into variable capital or additional labour-fund. If the scale of accumulation accelerates it may exceed the normal increase of labour-power or the number of labourers, and the demand for labour may exceed the supply, and therefore wages may rise.

A rise in the price of labour resulting from accumulation of capital implies two alternatives. Ether the price of labour keeps on rising, because its rise does not interfere with the progress of accumulation. In this case it is evident that a diminution in the unpaid labour in no way interferes with the extension of the domain of capital. Or on the other hand, accumulation slackens in consequence of the rise in the price of labour, because the stimulus of gain is blunted. The rate of accumulation lessens; but with its lessening, the primary cause of that lessening vanishes, i.e. the disproportion between capital and exploitable labour-power.

The mass of the means of production increases with the productiveness of labour. And these means of production play a double part. First more raw materials are worked up in the same time, along with auxiliary substances. This is a consequence of increasing productivity of labour. Second, the mass of machinery, buildings, furnaces, means of transport, etc. is a condition of the increasing productivity of labour.

There is an increase in the constant constituent of capital at the expense of its variable constituent. This law of the progressive increase in the constant capital, in proportion to variable, is confirmed at every step by a comparative analysis of the prices of commodities.

As well as accumulating, capital also becomes concentrated and centralised. It is the concentration of capitals already formed, the destruction of their individual independence. It is expropriation of capitalist by capitalist, transformation of many small into few large capitalists. With the development of the capitalist mode of production, there is an increase in the minimum amount of individual capital necessary to carry on a business under normal conditions. Competition rages amongst these smaller capitals, which crowd into spheres of production that modern industry has only sporadically or incompletely got hold of. It always ends in the ruin of many small capitalists, whose capitals partly pass into the hands of their rivals. Also as the credit system develops it soon becomes a new and terrible weapon in the battle of competition and is finally transformed into an enormous social mechanism for the centralisation of capitals.

In any given branch of industry centralisation would reach its extreme limit if all the individual capitals invested in it were fused into a single capital. In a given society the limit would be reached when the entire social capital was united in the hands of either a

31

single capitalist or a single capitalist company.

Joint-stock companies are formed and a more comprehensive organisation of collective work of many for a wider development of their material motive forces into processes of production socially combined and scientifically arranged.

Accumulation, the gradual increase of capital by reproduction as it passes from the circular to the spiral form, is clearly a very slow procedure compared with centralisation, which has only to change the quantitative groupings of the constituent parts of social capital. The world would still be without railways if it had needed to wait until accumulation had got a few individual capitals far enough to be adequate for the construction of a railway. (that was in the 1860s)

The additional capital formed in the course of accumulation attracts fewer and fewer labourers in proportion to its magnitude. The old capital periodically reproduced with change of competition, repels more and more of the labourers formerly employed by it.

Capitalist production can by no means content itself with the quantity of disposable labour-power which the natural increase in population yields. It requires for its free play an industrial reserve army independent of these natural limits. It is the absolute interest of every capitalist to press a given quantity of labour out of a smaller, rather than a greater number of labourers, if the cost is about the same, because the outlay of constant capital will be less for fewer labourers. The capitalist can also buy with the same capital a greater mass of labour-power, as he progressively replaces skilled labourers by less skilled.

If the means of production, as they increase in extent and effective power, become to a lesser extent the means of employment of labourers, this state of things is again modified by the fact that in proportion as the productiveness of labour increases, capital increases its supply of labour more quickly than the demand for labourers.

The over-work of the employed part of the

working class swells the ranks of the reserve, whilst conversely the greater pressure that the latter by its competition exerts on the former, forces these to submit to over-work and to subjugation under the dictates of capital.

The general movements of wages are exclusively regulated by the expansion and contraction of the industrial reserve army, and these again correspond to the periodic changes of the industrial cycle. The impulse that additional capital, seeking an outlet, would give to the general demand for labour is therefore in every case neutralised to the extent of the labourers thrown out of employment by the machine. In the centres of modern industry – factories, manufactories, ironworks, mines, etc. – the labourers are sometimes repelled, sometimes attracted again in greater masses with the number of those employed increasing on the whole, although in a constantly decreasing proportion to the scale of production.

In automatic factories, as in the great workshops, where machinery enters as a factor, large numbers of boys are employed up to the age of maturity. When this term is once reached, only a very small number continue to find employment in the same branches of industry.

The consumption of labour-power by capital is so rapid that the labourer, half-way through his life, has already more or less completely lived himself out. Within the capitalist mode of production all methods for raising the social productiveness of labour are brought about at the cost of the individual labourer. All means for the development of production transform themselves into the means of domination over, and exploitation of the producers. They mutilate the labourer into a fragment of a man, degrade him to the level of an appendage of a machine, destroy every remnant of charm in his work and turn it into a hated toil. They estrange from him the intellectual potentialities of the labour process in the same proportion as science is incorporated into it as an independent power. They distort the conditions under which he works, subject him during the labour-process to a despotism the more hateful for its meanness. They transform his life-time into working-time, and drag his wife and child beneath the wheels of the Juggernaut of capital.

The greater the centralisation of the means of production, the greater is the corresponding heaping together of labourers within a given space. The swifter capitalistic accumulation, the more miserable are the dwellings of working-people. "Improvements" of towns, accompanying the increase in wealth, by demolition of badly built quarters, the erection of palaces for banks, warehouses, etc. the widening of streets for business traffic, for the carriages of luxury, and for the introduction of tramways, etc. drive away the poor into ever worse and more crowded hiding places.

The owner of land, of houses, the businessman, when expropriated by "improvements" such as rail-roads, the building of new streets, etc. not only receives full indemnity, he must, according to law, human and divine, be comforted for his enforced

"Abstinence" over and above this by a thumping great profit.

The secret of primitive accumulation

In themselves money and commodities are no more capital than are means of production and of subsistence. They require transforming into capital. But this transformation can only take place under certain central conditions where two very different kinds of commodity possessors must come face to face and into contact. On the one hand, the owners of money, means of production, means of subsistence, who are eager to increase the sum of values they possess, by buying other peoples' labour-power and on the other hand, free labourers, the sellers of their own labour-power, and therefore the sellers of labour. Free labourers in a double sense - that neither they themselves form part and parcel of the means of production nor does the means of production belong to them, as in the case of peasant-proprietors. With this

37

polarisation of the market for commodities, the fundamental conditions of capitalist production are satisfied. As soon as the process of capitalist production is established, it not only maintains this separation, but reproduces it on a continually extended scale. The process, therefore, that clears the way for the capitalist system, can be none other than the process which takes away from the labourer the possession of his means of production. A process that transforms, on the one hand, the social means of subsistence and of production into capital and on the other, the immediate producers into wage-labourers. The economic structure of capitalistic society has grown out of the economic structure of feudal society. The dissolution of the latter set free the elements of the former. The new freed men became sellers of themselves only after they had been robbed of all their own means of production and of all guarantees of existence afforded by the old feudal arrangements.

The prelude of the revolution that laid the foundation of the capitalist mode of production was played in the last third of the 15th Century and the first decade of the 16th Century. In conflict with king and parliament, the great feudal lords created an incomparably large proletariat by the forcible driving of the peasantry from the land, to which the latter had the same feudal right as the lord himself and by the usurpation of the common land. The rapid rise of the Flemish wool manufacturers, and the corresponding rise in the price of wool in England, gave the direct impulse to these evictions.

The suppression of the monasteries at the time of the Reformation hurled their inmates into the proletariat. The estates of the Church were to a large extent given away to rapacious royal favourites or sold at a nominal price to speculating farmers and citizens, who drove out, en masse, the hereditary sub-tenants and threw their holdings into one. The legally guaranteed property of the poor folk in a part of the Church's tithes was tacitly confiscated. The parliamentary form of the robbery is that of acts for enclosures of commons. In other words, decrees by

39

which the landlords grant themselves the peoples' land as private property.

The system of public credit, i.e. of national debt, took possession of Europe generally during the manufacturing period. The only part of the so-called national wealth that actually enters into the collective possession of modern people is the national debt. The state-creditors give nothing away, for the sum lent is transferred into public bonds, easily negotiable, just as so much hard cash.

At their birth the great banks, decorated with national titles, were only associations of private speculators, who placed themselves by the side of governments, and, thanks to the privileges they received, were in a position to advance money to the state. Hence the accumulation of the national debt has no more infallible measure than the successive rise in the stock of these banks, whose full development dates from founding of the Bank of England in 1694. The Bank of England began by lending its money to the government at 8%. At the same time it was empowered by Parliament to coin money out of the same capital, by lending it again to the public in the form of banknotes. The wonder of banking! It was allowed to use these notes for discounting bills, making advances on commodities and for buying the precious metals. It was not long ere this credit-money, made by the bank itself, became the coin in which the Bank of England made its loans to the state, and paid, on account of the state, the interest on the public debt. Gradually it became inevitably the receptacle of the metallic hoard of the country and the centre of gravity of all commercial credit. This created a brood of bankocrats, financiers, rentiers, brokers, stock-jobbers, etc.

With the national debt arose an international credit system, which often conceals one of the sources of primitive accumulation. Thus the Venetians formed one of the secret bases of the capital-wealth of Holland to whom Venice lent large sums of money. Then one of the main lines of business of Holland from 1701 – 1776 is the lending out of enormous amounts of capital, especially to its great rival England.

The same thing went on during the 19th century between England and the United States.

The national debt finds its support in the public revenue, which must cover the yearly payments of interest etc. The modern system of taxation was the necessary complement of the system of national loans. The loans enable the government to meet extraordinary expenses, without the tax-payer feeling it immediately, but they necessitate, as a consequence, increased taxes. Taxes on the most necessary means of subsistence thus contains within itself the germ of automatic progression.

Historical tendency of capitalist accumulation

To perpetuate the system of small scale production that existed prior to the capitalist mode of production would be to "decree universal mediocrity". At a certain stage of development it brings forth the material agencies for its own dissolution. From the moment new forces and new passions spring up in the bosom of society the old social organisation fetters them and keeps them down. It must be annihilated. It is annihilated. The individualised and scattered means of production are transformed into socially concentrated ones, of pigmy property of many into the huge property of the few. The expropriation of the great mass of people from the soil and from the means of subsistence and from means of labour, this fearful and painful expropriation of the mass of the people forms the prelude to the history of capital.

As soon as this process of transformation has sufficiently decomposed the old society from top to bottom, as soon as the labourers are turned into proletarians, their means of labour into capital, as soon as the capitalist mode of production stands on its own feet, then the further socialisation of labour and further transformation of the land and other means of production into socially exploited and, therefore, common means of production, as well as the further expropriation of private proprietors, takes a new form. That which is now to be expropriated is no longer the labourer working for himself, but the capitalist exploiting many labourers. This expropriation is accomplished by the action of the immanent laws of capitalistic production itself and by the centralisation of capital. Hand in hand with this centralisation or this expropriation of many capitalists by few, there develops on an ever-extending scale, the co-operative form of the labour-process, the conscious technical application of science, the methodical cultivation of the soil, the transformation of the instruments of labour into instruments of labour only usable in common. The economising of all means of production by their use as the means of production of combined, socialised labour, the entanglement of all peoples in the net of the world-market, and with this, the international character of the capitalistic regime. Along with the constantly diminishing number of magnets of capital, who usurp and monopolise all advantages of this process of transformation the mass

44

of misery grows. Society experiences oppression, degradation, and exploitation. But with these grow the revolt of the working-class, a class always increasing in numbers, disciplined, united, and organised by the very mechanism of the process of capitalist production itself.

The monopoly of capital becomes a constraint upon the mode of production, which has sprung up and flourished along with and under it. The centralisation of the means of production and socialisation of labour at last reach a point where they become incompatible with their capitalist integument. This integument is burst asunder. The knell of capitalist private property sounds. The expropriators are expropriated. The capitalist mode of appropriation, the result of the capitalist mode of production, produces capitalist property. This is the first negation of individual private property, as founded on the labour of the proprietor. But capitalist production begets, with the inexorability of a law of nature, its own negation. This does not re-establish private property for the producer, but gives him individual property based on the acquisitions of the capitalist era: i.e. on co-operation and the possession in common of the land and means of production.

The transformation of scattered private property, arising from individual labour, into capitalistic private property is naturally, a process incomparably more protracted, violent and difficult than the transformation of capitalist private property, already practically resting on socialised production, into socialised property. In the former case, we had the expropriation of the mass of the people by a few usurpers. In the latter we have the expropriation of a few usurpers by the mass of the people.

The modern theory of colonisation

We have seen that expropriation of the mass of the people from the soil forms the basis of the capitalist mode of production. The essence of a free colony, on the contrary, requires that the bulk of the soil is still public property, and every settler on it therefore can turn part of it into his private property and individual means of production, without hindering the later settlers in the same operation. This is both the prosperity of the colonies and of their inveterate vice. Opposition to the establishment of capital. Where land is very cheap and all men are free, where every one who so pleases can easily obtain a piece of land for himself, not only is labour very dear, as respects the labourer's share of the produce, but the difficulty is to obtain combined labour at any price. So the government puts an artificial price on virgin soil in the colony, independent of the law of supply and demand, a price that compels the immigrant to work for wages before he can earn enough money to buy land, and turn himself into an independent peasant. The fund resulting from the sale of the land at a price prohibitory for wage-workers is employed by the government in proportion as it grows, to import have-nothings from Europe into the colonies and thus keep the wage-labour market full for the capitalists. This is the great secret of "systematic colonisation". The shameless lavishing of uncultivated colonial land on aristocrats and capitalists by the government has produced especially in Australia an ample relative surplus labouring population. Also, the stream of men that the gold-diggings attract, and the competition from imported English commodities augment this process.

As a result of this and pressure in Europe, the enormous and ceaseless stream of men, year after year driven to America, leaves behind a stationery sediment in the east of the United States, the wave of immigration from Europe throwing men on the labour-market there more rapidly than the wave of immigration westwards can wash them away.

Conclusion

The first volume describes the mechanics of the economic system as a machine that delivers wealth in the form of commodities at an increasing rate. The basic concept of the labour theory of value is demonstrated, which leads to the definition of money. Marx recognises that paper money must represent gold. Gold is the only reliable index for all commodities. Marx then describes the structure of the economic system. At certain times unusual circumstances can force prices (exchange value) to be extremely above or below their labour value, but the norm is to follow the labour value on average and in the long term. This is born out by the correlation between wages, prices and inflation. But these concepts are not openly accepted by some authorities, notably banks.

Marx seems to disapprove of surplus-value and never acknowledges it as a reward for supplying capital, or delayed consumption. He sees it only as being the result of the means of production being taken from the people then used to exploit them.

It is the continual re-investing of surplus-value that causes the economy to become more productive. This Marx does acknowledge. *"forces the human race to produce for productions' sake, he thus forces the development of the productive forces of society.....".* Even today the governments and banks, and most politicians say that the economy must expand. But why? Wouldn't long term sustainability be a better achievement?

Society is continually transforming itself, as wealth increases and capital becomes concentrated. *"The monopoly of capital becomes a fetter upon the mode of production......is burst asunder".* We may have reached this point now for the banks are only interested in making paper money gains without being concerned with any other factors. Funds are not guided into sustainable investments by being lent to business and industry, but put into all manner of dubious schemes. This is also coupled with printing or creating money so causing inflation and the ultimate break-down of the financial system. Could the current financial crisis, caused by the banking sector decoupling from business and industry be the point of transformation (*bursting asunder*). The Bolshevik revolution of 1917 did not have these characteristics and finally failed. It's failure also demonstrating that centrally planned economies have serious short comings. Restricting decision making to a small group of people looses the mass of information that would be forthcoming from the whole population. The way the banks are now behaving undermines the functioning of free-markets. Quantitative easing is undermining the currencies and removes the use of a savings account to make a store of value. It effectively steals money from your account with every addition to the money supply.

Because of the problems with the Euro, some states may revert to their previous currencies, but are reluctant to do so because they require a universal currency for European trade. There is a universal inflation proof currency. It is gold. The solution would be to go onto a gold standard. Each state could then choose to use it's own currency, as long as it was backed by gold. This would stop the banks and governments running the affairs of the country as a giant ponzi scheme.   51

BOOK 2

The process

of

Circulation of Capital

The circuit of money capital

The circular movement of capital takes place in three stages:

First stage: The capitalist appears as a buyer on the commodity and labour market, and his money is transformed into commodities, or it goes through the circulation act $M \rightarrow C$.

Second stage: Productive consumption of the commodities purchased by the capitalist now takes place. He acts as a capitalist producer of commodities, and his capital passes through the process of production. The result is a commodity of more value than that of the elements entering into its production.

Third stage: The capitalist returns to the market as a seller, and his commodities are turned into money, or they pass through the circulation act $C \rightarrow M$.

Hence the formula for money-capital is:
$M \rightarrow C \ldots P \ldots C' \rightarrow M'$, the dots indicating that the

process of circulation is interrupted, and C' and M' designating C and M increased by surplus-value.

It is taken for granted here that commodities are sold at their value and it does not change throughout the process. This formula for the circuit of money-capital is the matter-of–course form of the circuit of capital only on the basis of already developed capitalist production, because it presupposes the existence of a class of wage-labourers on a social scale.

The circuit of capital being considered here begins with the act M $\rightarrow$ C, i.e. the purchase of commodities. Circulation must therefore be complemented by the antithetical metamorphosis C $\rightarrow$ M, the transformation of commodities into money or sales. By the transformation of money-capital into productive capital the capital value has acquired a bodily form in which it cannot continue to circulate but must enter into consumption, that is, into productive consumption.

$$M \rightarrow C \rightarrow L \quad = \text{labour-power}$$
$$\rightarrow MP \quad = \text{means of production}$$

The use of labour-power, can be materialised only in the labour process. The quantity of labour must match the quantity of means of production to be efficient.

$M \rightarrow L$. The wage labourer lives only by the sale of his labour-power. The preservation, his self-preservation, requires daily consumption. Hence payment for it must be continually repeated at rather short intervals in order that he may be able to repeat the acts $L \rightarrow M \rightarrow C$ or (labour-power being a commodity) $C \rightarrow M \rightarrow C$, repeat the purchases needed for his self-preservation.

For this reason the capitalist must always meet the wage-labourer in the capacity of a money-capitalist. On the other hand if the wage-labourers are to perform the act $L \rightarrow M \rightarrow C$, they must constantly be faced with the necessary means of subsistence in purchasable form, i.e. in the form of commodities.

This state of affairs necessitates a high degree of development of the circulation of products in the form of commodities, hence also of the volume of commodities produced. $M \rightarrow MP$ develops to the same extent as $M \rightarrow L$, that is to say the production of means of production come from branches of production that specialise in such commodities. In purchasing means of production as commodities the capitalist must assume the role of money-capitalist, in other words there is an increase in the scale of which his capital must assume the functions of money-capital. Whereas labour-power is a commodity only in the hands of its sellers, the wage-labourer, it became capital only in the hands of the buyer, the capitalist who acquires the temporary use of it. The means of production does not become material forms of productive capital, until labour-power, the personal form of existence of productive capital, is capable of being embodied in them. Human labour-power is by nature no more capital than are means of production. They acquire this specific

4

social character only under definite, historically developed conditions, just as only under such conditions the character of money is stamped upon precious metals, or that of money-capital upon that of money.

The function of C' is now that of all commodities, to transform itself into money, to be sold and to go through the circulation stage C → M. So long as the capital, now expanded, remains in the form of commodity capital and lies immovable in the market, the process of production is at rest. The commodity-capital acts neither as a creator of products nor a creator of value.

The circuit M → C ... P ... C' → M', in its expanded form, is therefore represented by

$$M \to C \to L \quad \ldots P \ldots (C+c) \to (M+m)$$
$$\to MP.$$

In the first stage the capitalist takes articles of consumption out of the commodity-market proper and the labour-market. In the third stage it throws commodities back, but only into the commodity-market proper. However he extracts more value from the market than he threw in originally due to throwing more commodity-value back upon it than he first drew out of it. It becomes important in the process of the reproduction of capital, depending on whether m is entirely or partially or not at all lumped together with M, i.e. depending on whether or not it continues to function as a component part of the advanced capital-value. Both M and m may pass through quite different processes of circulation. The two forms assumed by capital-value at the various stages of its circulation are those of *money-capital* and *commodity-capital*.

The form pertaining to the stage of production is that of *productive-capital*. The capital which assumes these forms in the course of its total circuit is *industrial-capital*.

Capital describes its circuits normally only so long as its various phases pass uninterruptedly into one another. If capital stops short in its first phase M → C, money-capital assumes the rigid form of a hoard; if it stops in the phase of production, the means of production lie idle, and the labour-power remains unemployed; and if capital is stopped short in its last phase C' → M', piles of unsold commodities accumulate and clog the flow of circulation.

It has been assumed that the entire capital-value advanced in the form of money passes in bulk from one stage to the next. But we have seen that a part of the constant capital, the labour instruments proper (e.g. machinery), constantly serve anew, with more or less numerous repetitions of the same processes of production, hence transfer their values piecemeal to the products. It will be seen later to what extent this circumstance modifies the circular movement of capital. There are certain branches of industry in which the product of the productive process is not a new material product nor is it commodity, the communications industry being an example.

The third stage C' → M' is a sale on one part, but is M → C, a purchase, on the other part. In the last analysis a commodity is bought only for its use-value, in order to enter the process of consumption, whether this is individual or productive.

In the case of the purchase of means of production and in the sale of produced commodities money figures in the form of money of account and finally in cash only in the balancing of accounts.

I. Simple reproduction

For simple reproduction of productive capital we assume conditions remain constant and commodities are bought and sold at their value. In this case the entire surplus-value enters into the individual consumption of the capitalist. The remainder of C' being the capital-value continues to circulate in the circuit of industrial capital.

$$
\begin{array}{ccc}
& & L \\
& M & \to \quad MP \\
C' = (C + c) & \to \quad M' = & + \\
& m & \to \quad c
\end{array}
$$

8

If the commodities C' are sold to a merchant, the M, money-capital remains in the productive circuit, but the commodities move into the sphere of general circulation. While c → m, the surplus-value being spent as revenue (m → c), enters into general circulation as individual consumption of the capitalist.

In order that the circuit be completed normally, C' must be sold at its value and in its entirety. Further more C → M → C includes not merely replacements of one commodity by another, but replacement with value-relations remaining the same. We assume that this takes place here. However, the values of means of production vary. It is precisely capitalist production to which continuous change of value-relations is peculiar, if only because of the ever changing productivity of labour that characterizes this mode of production.

If the metamorphosis, M' → C, meets with any obstacles – for instance if there are no means of production in the market – the circuit, the flow of

9

the process of production is interrupted quite as much as when capital is held fast in the form of commodity-capital. But there is this difference. It can remain longer in the money-form than in the transitory form of commodities. It does not cease to be money if it does not perform the functions of money-capital. But it does cease to be a commodity or use-value in general, if it is delayed to long in the exercise of its function of commodity-capital.

Furthermore, in its money-form it is capable of assuming another form in place of its original one of productive capital, while it cannot budge at all if held in the form of C'.

If C' continues to circulate for instance in the hands of the merchant who bought it, this at first does not in the least affect the continuation of the circuit of the individual capital that produced it. The entire process continues and with it the individual consumption of the capitalist and labourer made necessary by it. This point is important in a discussion of crises.

The quantity of commodities created in masses by capitalist production depends on the scale of production and on the need for constantly expanding this production, and not on a predestined circle of supply and demand and on wants that have to be satisfied. Mass production can have no other direct buyer, apart from other industrial capitalists, than the wholesaler. Within certain limits, the process of reproduction may take place on the same scale or on an increased scale even when the commodities expelled from it did not really enter individual or productive consumption. So long as the product is sold, everything is taking its regular course from the standpoint of the capitalist producer. The circuit of the capital-value he is identified with is not interrupted. And if this process is expanded, which includes increased productive consumption of means of production and this reproduction of capital may be accompanied by increased individual consumption (hence demand) on the part of labourers, since this process is initiated and

11

effected by productive consumption. The entire process of reproduction may be in a flourishing condition and yet a large part of the commodities may have entered into consumption only apparently, while in reality they may still remain unsold in the hands of dealers and may in fact still be lying in the market.

Now one stream of commodities follows another and finally it is discovered that the previous streams have been absorbed only apparently by consumption. The commodity capitals compete with one another for a place in the market. Late comers, to sell at all, sell at lower prices. The former streams have not yet been disposed of when payment for them falls due. Their owners must declare their insolvency or sell at any price to meet their obligations. This sale has nothing whatever to do with the actual state of demand. It only concerns the *demand for payment*, the pressing necessity of transforming commodities into money.

Then a crisis breaks out. It becomes visible not in the direct decrease of consumer demand, but in the decrease of exchanges of capital for capital i.e. of the reproductive process of capital.

II.   Accumulation and reproduction
on an extended scale

Since the proportions which the expansion of the productive process may assume are not arbitrary but prescribed by technology, the realised surplus-value, though intended for capitalization, frequently only after several successive circuits attains a size as will suffice for effective functioning as additional capital. The surplus-value congeals into a hoard in the form of silver or gold. It could also be held in the form of creditors' claims etc. It does not enter into the reproductive process of the circuit any more than does money invested in interest-bearing securities etc. although it may enter into the circuits of other individual industrial capitals. It is immaterial whether a certain surplus-value produced in any particular period is entirely

13

consumed or entirely capitalized. On the average –
and the general formula can represent only the
average movement – both cases occur. But in order
no to complicate the formula, it is better to
assume that the entire surplus-value is accumulated.
The formula:

$$P \ldots C' \to M' \to C' \to L \ldots P'$$
$$\to MP$$

stands for productive capital, which is reproduced on
an enlarged scale and with greater value. In the stage

$$M' \to C' \to L$$
$$\to MP$$

the augmented magnitude is indicated only by C',
but not L' or MP'. C' indicates sufficiently that the
sum of L and MP contained in it is greater than the
original P. But L' and MP' would be incorrect,
because the growth of capital involves a change in
the constitution of its value and as this change
progresses the value of MP increases, and that of L
always decreases relatively and often absolutely.

III. Accumulation of money

If m is to serve as money-capital in a second independent business or used to expand the original business, the relations between the material factors of P and their value-relations demand a minimum magnitude for m. In the interim m is accumulated and exits only in the shape of a hoard in process of formation of growth. Hence the accumulation of money, hoarding, appears here as a process by which real accumulation, the extension of scale on which industrial capital operates, is temporarily accompanied. Temporarily, for so long as the hoard remains in the condition of a hoard, it does not function as capital, does not take part in the process of creating surplus-value, remains a sum of money which grows only because money, come by without doing anything, is thrown into the same coffer.

The accumulation of money can be in the form of a hoard. It may also exist in the form of mere outstanding money, of claims on debtors by capitalists who have sold C'. As for other forms in which this latent money-capital may exist in the meantime even in the shape of money-breeding money, such as interest-bearing bank deposits, bills of exchange or securities of any description. These do not belong here. Surplus-value realised in the form of money in such cases performs special capital-functions outside the circuit described by the industrial capital which originated it – functions which in the first place have nothing to do with that circuit as such but which in the second place presuppose capital-functions which differ from the functions of industrial capital and which have not yet been developed here.

IV. Reserve fund

The accumulation-fund can also perform special services, of a subordinate nature, and enter into the capital circuit without an expansion of capitalist production. If the commodity-capital is abnormally delayed in its transformation into the money-form or if, for instance, the price of means of production has risen, the hoard functioning as accumulation-fund can be used as part of the money-capital.

Thus the money accumulation fund serves as a reserve fund for counter-balancing disturbances in the circuit. In the continuous process of production, reserve-money capital is always formed. Since one day money is received and no payments have to be made until later, and another day large quantities of goods are sold while other large quantities are not due to be bought until a subsequent date. In these intervals a part of the circulating capital exists continuously in the form of money. A reserve fund is not a constituent part of capital already performing its functions, or, to be more exact money-capital. It is rather a part of capital in a preliminary stage of its accumulation of surplus-value not yet transformed into active capital. A capitalist in financial straits does not concern himself with the particular functions of the money he has on hand. He simply employs whatever money he has for the purpose of keeping his capital circulating.

The circuit of commodity-capital

It is only in the circuit described by C' itself that C equal to P and equal to the capital value, can and must separate from that part of C' in which surplus-value exists, from the surplus-product in which the surplus-value is lodged. It does not matter whether the two things can be actually separated, as in the case of yarn, or whether they cannot, as in the case of a machine. They always become separable as soon as C' is transformed into M'. The surplus-value does not circulate until later. The capitalist could get through

$$C \rightarrow M \rightarrow C \rightarrow L$$
$$\rightarrow MP$$

before the circulation of the surplus-product

$C > m > c$ is accomplished.

$$
\begin{array}{l}
 \to L \\
M \to C \to MP \ldots P \ldots C' \\
C' = (C + c) \to M' \to + \\
 m \to c
\end{array}
$$

The circuit C' ... C' presupposes within its sphere, the existence of other industrial capital in the form of $C = L + MP$: and MP comprises diverse other capitals, such as machinery, coal, oil, etc. This *general* form of the circuit in which every single industrial capital can be studied, can be extended as a form of movement of the sum of the individual capitals i.e. the aggregate capital of the capitalist class. A movement in which that of each individual industrial capital appears as only a partial movement which intermingles with the other movements and is necessitated by them. For instance if we regard the aggregate of commodities annually produced in a certain country and analyse the movement by which a part of it replaces the productive capital in all

19

individual businesses, while another part enters into individual consumption of various classes. Then we consider C' ... C' as a form of movement of social capital as well as of the surplus-value, or surplus-product, generated by it. The social capital is equal to the sum of the individual capitals (including the joint-stock capital or the state capital, so far as governments employ productive wage-labour in mines, railways, etc., perform the function of industrial capitalists), and that the aggregate movement of social capital is equal to the algebraic sum of the movements of the individual capitals. This method of analysis presents other phenomena and helps to provide solutions to some problems.

Reproduction on an extended scale with productivity remaining constant. This can only take place when the part of the surplus-product to be capitalized already contains the material elements of the additional productive capital. So far as the production of one year serves as the premise of the following year's production or so far as this can take place simultaneously with the process of simple reproduction within one year, the surplus-product is at once produced in a form which enables it to perform the functions of additional capital. Increased productivity can increase only the substance of capital but not its value but therein it creates additional material for the self-expansion of that value.

The three formulas of the circuit

The three formulas $M > P > C' > M'$
$P > C > M > P$
$C > M > P > C'$,

are happening simultaneously. To see what happens in reality. While, e.g. 10,000 lbs of yarn appear in the market as commodity-capital and are transformed into money, new cotton is being converted from the money form and begins to function as productive capital. All parts of capital successively describe

21

circuits and are simultaneously at its different stages. The industrial capital, continuously progressing along its orbit, thus exists simultaneously at all stages and in the diverse functional forms corresponding to these stages. The circuit of industrial capital in its continuity is the unity of all its three circuits. The magnitude of the available capital determines the dimensions of the process of production and this again determines the dimensions of the commodity-capital and money-capital in so far as they perform their functions parallel with the process of production. However, co-existence, by which continuity of production is determined, is only due to the movement of those parts of capital in which they successively pass through their different stages. Co-existence is itself merely the result of succession. If for instance C' → M' stagnates as far as one part is concerned, if the commodity cannot be sold, then the circuit of this part is interrupted and no replacement by its means of production takes place. The succeeding parts, which emerge from the process of

22

production in the shape of C', find the change of their function blocked by their predecessors. If this lasts for some time, production is restricted and the entire process brought to a halt.

If social capital experiences a revolution in value, it may happen that the capital of the individual capitalist succumbs to it and fails because it cannot adapt itself to the conditions of this movement of values. The more acute and frequent such revolutions in value become, disrupting the course of normal production which becomes subservient to abnormal speculation, the greater the danger that threatens the existence of the individual capitals.

The process takes a wholly normal course only when the value-relations remain constant. But the greater these disturbances the greater the money-capital which the industrial capitalist must posses to tide over the period of readjustment, and as the scale of each individual process of production and with it the minimum size of capital to be advanced increases in the process of capitalist production, we have here another circumstance to be added to those others which transform the function of the industrial capitalist more and more into a monopoly of big money-capitalists, who may operate singly or in association.

The greater the velocity of the currency of money, the more rapidly therefore every individual capital passes through the series of its commodity or money metamorphosis and the more numerous are the industrial capitals starting to circulate successively by a given mass of money. The more the money functions as a paying medium for instance in the replacement of its' means of production by its' commodity-capital, nothing but balances have to be squared, and the shorter the periods of time when payments fall due. The less money a given mass of capital-value therefore requires for its circulation. On the other hand, assuming that the velocity of circulation and all other conditions remain the same, the amount of money required to circulate as money-capital is determined by the sum of the prices of the commodities, or if the quantity and value of the commodities are fixed, by the value of the money itself. Natural economy, money-economy and credit-economy have been placed in opposition to one another as being the three characteristic economic forms of movement in social production.

The capitalist throws less value in the form of money into the circulation than he draws out of it, because he throws into it more value in the form of commodities than he withdrew from it in the form of commodities.

Since the labourer generally converts his wages into means of subsistence, the demand of the capitalist for labour-power is indirectly also a demand for articles of consumption essential to the working-class. The upper limit of the capitalist's demand is C, equal to $c + v$, but his supply is $c + v + s$.

To investigate the problem of turnover, let the total capital of the capitalist be £5,000, of which

£4,000 is fixed and £1,000 circulating capital; let this £1,000 be composed of 800c and 200v, producing 200s. His circulating capital must be turned over five times a year for his total capital to turn over once. His commodity-product is then equal to £6,000 i.e. £1,000 more than his advanced capital. Suppose his fixed capital has to be renewed in 10 years. So the capitalist pays every year one-tenth, or £400, into a sinking fund and thus has a value of £3,600 of fixed capital left plus £400 in money.

While capital is accumulating in the form of a hoard it does not increase the demand of the capitalist. The money is immobilized. It does not withdraw from the commodity-market any equivalent in commodities for the money-equivalent withdrawn from it for commodities supplied.

The time of circulation

The time of production of the means of production in general comprises :-

1. the time during which they function as means of production, hence serve in the productive process;

2. the stops during which the process of production is interrupted;

3. the time during which they are held in readiness as prerequisites of the process.

The normal interruptions of the entire process of production, the intermissions during which the productive capital does not function, create neither value nor surplus-value. However, the value of the constant part of capital, which continues in the productive process although the labour-process is interrupted, re-appears in the result of the productive process. It is plain that the more the production time and labour-time cover each other the greater is the productivity and self expansion of a given productive capital in a given space of time. Hence the tendency of capitalist production to reduce the excess of the production time over the labour-time as much as possible.

Time of circulation and time of production mutually exclude each other. During its time of circulation capital does not perform the functions of productive capital and therefore produces neither commodities nor surplus-value. Use-values are perishable by nature. Hence if they are not productively or individually consumed within a certain time, they spoil and lose their use-value and the property of being vehicles of exchange-value. The capital-value contained in them is lost hence the loss of surplus-value accrued in it.

The costs of circulation

The functions of buying and selling are part of the cost of circulation and do not add value to the product. The book-keeping, the tracing of values and materials throughout the productive process incur costs but do not add value. Money is essential for the circulation of commodities and gold and silver coins wear down and have to be replaced. This is part of the cost of circulation. Paper money also wears and has to be reprinted.

The duration of a turnover is determined by the sum of its time of production and its time of circulation. A circuit performed by a capital and meant to be a periodic process, is called a turnover. A year is the natural unit for measuring the turnovers of a functioning capital, denoted by T, and if the time of turnover of a given capital is given as t, and the number of turnovers by n, then n = T/t.

Fixed capital and circulating capital

Part of the constant capital may function during several turnovers before it is completely worn out, and only a fraction of its value passes to the product during each turnover. During the entire period of its functioning, a part of its value always remains fixed in it; independently of the commodities it helps to produce. This part of constant capital is called *fixed capital*.

Some means of production do not enter materially into the product, being auxiliary materials such as coal or oil or gas. It is only their value which forms a part of the value of the products. The product circulates in its own circulation the value of these means of production. It is only the functioning of a product as an instrument of labour in the process of production that makes it fixed capital. But when it itself emerges from a process, it is by no means fixed capital. For instance a machine, as a product or commodity of the machine-manufacturer, belongs to his commodity-capital. It does not become fixed capital until it is employed productively in the hands of its purchaser, the capitalist. Fixed capital takes such forms as factory buildings, blast furnaces, canals, railways, ships, etc. Instruments of labour attached to the soil by their roots cannot be sent abroad, cannot circulate as commodities in the world-markets. Title to this fixed capital may change, it may be bought and sold, and to this extent may circulate ideally. These titles of ownership may even circulate in foreign markets, for instance in the form of stocks.

The peculiar circulation of fixed capital results in a peculiar turnover. That part of the value which it loses in its bodily form by wear and tear circulates as a part of the value of the product. The product converts itself by means of circulation from commodities into money. If a machine worth £10,000 lasts for, a period of ten years, then the period of turnover of the value originally advanced for it amounts to ten years. During the ten years its value circulates piecemeal as a part of the value of the commodities whose continuous production it serves and it is thus gradually transformed into money until finally at the end of ten years it entirely assumes the form of money and is reconverted from money into a machine, in other words, has completed its turnover.

The mass of fixed capital invested in a certain bodily form and endowed in the form with a certain average life constitutes one reason for the only gradual pace of introduction of new machinery, etc., and therefore an obstacle to the rapid general introduction of improvements of labour. On the other hand competition compels the replacement of the old instruments of labour by new ones before the expiration of their natural life, especially when decisive changes occur. Such premature renewals of factory equipment on a rather large social scale are mainly enforced by catastrophes or crisis.By means of a sinking fund, in which the value of the fixed capital flows back to its starting-point in proportion to its wear and tear, a part of the circulating money again forms a hoard, for a longer or shorter period, in the hands of the same capitalist whose hoard had, upon the purchase of the fixed capital, been transformed into a medium of circulation and passes away from him. It is a continually changing distribution of the hoard which exists in society and alternately functions as a medium of circulation and then is separated again, as a hoard, from the mass of circulating money. With the development of the credit-system, this money no longer serves as a hoard but as capital; however not in the hands of its owner but of other capitalists at whose disposal it has been placed.

The aggregate turnover of advanced capital
Cycles of turnover

It follows that even if by far the greater part of the advanced productive capital consists of fixed capital whose period of reproduction, hence also turnover, comprises a cycle of many years, the capital-value turned over during the year may, on account of the repeated turnovers of the circulating capital within the same year, be larger than the aggregate value of the advanced capital. Suppose the fixed capital is £80,000 and its period of reproduction of 10 years, so that £8,000 of it annually return to money-form, or it completes one-tenth of its turnover. Suppose further the circulating capital is £20,000, and its turnover is completed five times per year. The total capital would then be £100,000. The turned-over of fixed capital is £8,000, the turned-over of circulating capital five times £20,000, or £100,000. Then the capital turned over during one year is £108,000 or £8,000 more than the the advanced capital.

Though the durability of the applied fixed capital may last for many years, say ten years on average, the continuous revolution in means of production, involves changes necessitating their constant replacement on account of moral depreciation, long before they expire physically.

The cycle of interconnected turnovers embracing a number of years, in which the capital is held fast by its fixed constituent part, furnishes a material basis for the periodic crises. During this cycle business undergoes successive periods of depression, medium activity, precipitancy and crisis. Periods in which capital is invested differ greatly and far from coincide in time. But a crisis always forms the starting-point of large new investments. Therefore, from the point of view of society as a whole, more or less, a new material basis for the next turnover cycle.

The turnover of the variable capital from the Social point of view

The need of society to calculate beforehand how much labour, means of production and means of subsistence it can invest, without detriment, in such lines of business as for instance the building of railways, which do not furnish any means of production or subsistence, nor produce any useful effect for a long time, a year or more, while they extract labour, means of production and means of subsistence from the total annual production. So great disturbances may and must constantly occur. On the one hand pressure is brought to bear on the money-market, while on the other, an easy money-market calls such enterprises into being *en masse,* thus creating the very circumstances which later give rise to pressure on the money-market. Pressure is brought to bear on the money-market, since large advances of money-capital are constantly needed here for long periods of time.

Since elements of productive capital are for ever being withdrawn from the market and only an equivalent in money is thrown on the market in their place, the effective demand rises without itself furnishing any element of supply. Hence a rise in the prices of productive materials as well as means of subsistence.

They create a strong demand for articles of consumption on the market. Wages rise at the same time. Imports grow to meet demand and branches of industry in which production can be rapidly expanded, do so, soon followed by collapse. The labour-market goes from great demand to being depressed.

The circulation of surplus value

The expansion of the scale of production may proceed in small portions, a part of the surplus-value being used for improvements which either simply increase the productive power of the labour employed or permit the same time of its more intensive exploitation. Along with the real accumulation or conversion of surplus-value into productive capital, there is, then, an accumulation of money, a raking together of a portion of the surplus-value in the form of latent money-capital, which is not intended to function as additional active capital until later, when it swells to a certain volume. The money-capital which the capitalist cannot as yet employ in his own business is employed by others, who pay him interest for its use.

The simplest form in which the additional latent money-capital may be represented is that of a hoard. It may be that this hoard is additional gold or silver secured directly or indirectly in exchange with countries producing precious metals. And only in this manner does the hoarded money in a country grow absolutely. On the other hand it may be – and is so in the majority of cases – that this hoard is nothing but money which has been withdrawn from circulation at home and has assumed the form of a hoard in the hands of individual capitalists. It is also possible that this latent money-capital consists only of tokens of value – or mere claims of capitalists against third persons conferred by legal documents.

The wealth that is annually consumed, disappearing with its consumption, is seen but for a moment, and makes no impression except during the act of enjoyment or use. But that part of wealth which is of slow consumption, furniture, machinery, buildings, from childhood to old age, stand out before the eye, the durable monuments of human exertion. By means of the possession of this fixed, permanent or slowly consumed part of national wealth, of land and materials to work upon, the tools to work with, the houses to shelter, the holders of these articles command for their own benefit the yearly productive powers of all the really productive labourers of society, though these articles may bear ever so small a proportion to the recurring products of that labour. The whole amount of accumulated capital has been estimated at about three times the year's labour of the community.

About one-third part of the annual products of the labour is abstracted from the producers, under the name of public burdens, and unproductively consumed by those who give no equivalent, that is to say, none satisfactory to the producers.

As nothing can be accumulated without first supplying necessaries, and as the great current of human inclination is to enjoyment; hence the comparatively trifling amount of actual wealth of society at any particular moment. 'Tis an eternal round of production and consumption.

Simple reproduction

The total quantity of money is always equal to the sum of the money hoarded and the money circulating. A portion of this hoard is consumed by wear and tear,. It must be replaced annually. If the sum of the values of the annually produced and circulating quantity of commodities increases, the annual production of gold and silver must likewise increase, inasmuch as the increased sum of the values of the circulating commodities and the quantity of money required for their circulation (and the corresponding formation of a hoard) are not made good by a greater velocity of money currency and a more comprehensive function of money as medium of payment, i.e. by a greater mutual balancing of purchases and sales without the intervention of actual money.

For the capitalists who are engaged in the production of gold and silver, the money-form of the circulating capital consumed in labour-power and means of production is replaced, not by the sale of the product, but by the bodily form of the product itself; hence, not by once more withdrawing its value from circulation in money-form, but by additional newly produced money. This money thrown into circulation for labour and means of production does not return to its starting point.

The commodity-capital, which the capitalist throws into circulation, has a greater value than the productive capital which he withdrew from circulation in the form of labour-power plus means of production. So where does the money come from to convert the surplus-value from its commodity form? The capitalist class itself throws the money into circulation which serves for the realisation of the surplus-value incorporated in the commodities. It does not throw it into circulation as advanced money, hence not as capital. It spends it as a means of purchase for its individual consumption, say during the first turnover of its advanced capital; this is its point of departure of its circulation. At the end of the turnover the surplus-value in the form of commodities returns and can be converted into money, and so returns to its point of departure. This is obviously an arbitrary assumption so far as the individual capitalist is concerned. But it must be correct when applied to the entire capitalist class if simple reproduction is assumed.

The capitalists producing gold possess their entire product in gold – that portion which replaces constant as well as that which replaces variable capital, and also that consisting of surplus-value. Hence, whereas one part of the capitalist class throws into circulation commodities greater in value than the money-capital advanced by them, another part of the capitalists throws into circulation money of greater value (greater by the amount of the surplus-value) than that of the commodities which they constantly withdraw from circulation for the production of gold.

Accumulation and reproduction
on an extended scale

With reproduction on an extended scale, where does the additional money come from with which to realize the additional surplus-value now contained in the form of commodities? The sum total of the prices of the circulating commodities has been increased, because the mass of the commodities now circulating is greater than that of the previously circulating commodities. The additional money required for the circulation of this greater quantity of commodities of greater value must be secured either by greater economy in the use of the circulating quantity of money – whether by balancing of payments, etc., by measures which accelerate the circulation of the same coins – or by the transformation of money from the form of a hoard into that of a circulating medium.

When these measures do not suffice, additional gold must be produced, or, what amounts to the same, a part of the additional product exchanged, directly or indirectly, for gold – the product of countries in which precious metals are mined. To the extent that the costs of this expensive machinery of circulation are decreased, the given scale of production or the given degree of extension remaining constant, the productive power of social labour is increased. Hence, so far as expediencies developing with the credit system have this effect, they increase capitalist wealth directly, either by performing a large portion of social production and labour-process without any intervention of real money, or by raising the functional capacity of the quantity of money really functioning.

One part of the capitalists accumulates their surplus-value in the shape of money, forms latent money-capital, while the other part accumulates genuinely, that is to say, enlarges the scale of production. The available quantity of money remains sufficient for the requirements of circulation, even if, alternately, one part of capitalists accumulates money, while the other enlarges the scale of production, and vice versa.

The fund for circulation, the latent money-capital, which is accumulated for future use, consists:

1.   Of deposits in banks; and it is a comparatively trifling sum which is really at the disposal of the bank. Money-capital is accumulated here only nominally. What is actually accumulated is

outstanding claims which can be converted into money (if ever) only because a certain balance arises between the money withdrawn and the money deposited. It is only a relatively small sum that the bank holds in its hands in money.

2.   Of government securities. These are not capital at all, but merely outstanding claims on the annual product of the nation.

3.   Of stocks. Titles of ownership of some corporative real capital and drafts on the surplus-value accruing annually from it.

The reproduction and circulation
of the aggregate social capital

Simple reproduction

The question that confronts us directly is this: How is the *capital* consumed in production replaced in value out of the annual product and how does the movement of this replacement intertwine with the consumption of the surplus-value by the capitalists and the wages of the labourers? It is then first a matter of reproduction on a simple scale. It is furthermore assumed that products are exchanged at their values and also that there is no revolution in the values of the component parts of productive capital. As far as accumulation does take place, simple reproduction is always a part of it, and can therefore be studied by itself and is an actual factor of accumulation.

The two departments of social reproduction

The total product, and therefore the total production of society, may be divided into two major departments:

I. *Means of production*, commodities having a form in which they must, or at least may, pass into productive consumption.

II. *Articles of consumption*, commodities having a form in which they pass into the individual

46

consumption of the capitalist and working-class.

In each department the capital consists of two parts:

1. *Variable capital.* This capital, so far as its *value* is concerned, is equal to the value of the social labour-power employed in this branch of production; in other words, it is equal to the sum of the wages paid for this labour-power.

2. *Constant capital.* This is the value of all the means of production employed for productive purposes in this branch. These again, are divided into *fixed* capital, such as machines, instruments of labour, buildings, etc., and *circulating* constant capital, such as materials of production: raw and auxiliary materials, semi-finished products, etc.

For this analysis fixed capital will be ignored. The entire annual product of each department consists of c (constant) + v (variable) + s (surplus-value), and the rate of surplus-value s/v to be 100 per cent.

Production of Means of Production:

Capital

$$4,000c + 1,000v = 5,000$$

Commodity-Product

$4,000c + 1,000v + 1,000s = 6,000$ in means of
production.

Production of Articles of Consumption:

Capital

$$2,000c + 500v = 2,500$$

Commodity-Product

$2,000c + 500v + 500s = 3,000$ in articles of
consumption

Total value 9,000, exclusive of fixed capital
persisting in its natural form, according to our
assumption. If we now examine the transformations

necessary on the basis of simple reproduction, where the entire surplus-value is unproductively consumed, we obtain three points of support.

1. The 500v, representing wages of the labourers, and 500s, representing surplus-value of the capitalists, in department II, must be spent for articles of consumption. Consequently the wages and surplus-value of department II are exchanged within this department for products of this same department.

2. The 1,000v plus 1,000s of department I must likewise be spent for articles of consumption; in other words, for products of department II. Hence they must be exchanged for the remainder of this product equal to the constant capital part, 2,000c. Department II receives in return an equal quantity of means of production the product of I.

3. There still remain 4,000c. These consist of means of production of means of production which can be used only in department I to replace its consumed constant capital, and are therefore disposed of by mutual exchange between individual capitalists of I.

49

It follows that, on the basis of simple reproduction, the sum of the values of v + s of the commodity capital of I must be equal to the constant capital IIc.

The mediation of exchange
by the circulation of money

The circulation between the various classes is indicated in the following scheme:

Between class I and class II:

I.   4,000c + 1,000v + 1,000s

II.   2,000c   + 500v + 500s

This disposes of the circulation of IIc, equal to 2,000, which is exchanged for I (1,000v + 1,000s).

Category II of the annual production of commodities can be divided into two great sub-divisions by their products:

Articles of consumption that are the *necessities*

of life, we will call type *a*, and articles of luxury, we will call type *b*.

Now if II(v+s) is divided between the sub-classes IIa and IIb in the following manner:

II. $500v + 500s = a(400v + 400s) + b(100v + 100s)$

The capitalists of both sub-classes spend three-fifths of their surplus-value in products of IIa (necessities) and two-fifths in products of IIb (luxuries). The scheme for this is therefore:

IIa. [400v] + [240s] + 160s

IIb   100v + 60s   + [40s]

The bracketed items circulating are being consumed only within their own sub-class.

Money advanced to the circulation by producers of commodities returns to them in the normal course of commodity circulation. It follows that if any money capitalist advances to the industrial capitalist money-capital, the real point of reflux for this money is the money capitalist. Thus the mass of the circulating money belongs to that department of money-capital which is organized and concentrated by the banks.

The circulation of commodities always requires two things: Commodities which are thrown into circulation and money which is likewise thrown into it. The money does not vanish on dropping out of the circuit of the metamorphosis of a given commodity. It is constantly being precipitated into new places in the arena of circulation vacated by other commodities.

For instance in the circulation between IIc and I(v+s) we assume that II advances £500 in money for it. In the innumerable processes of circulation, into which the circulation between large social groups resolves itself, representatives of the various groups will at various times be the first to appear as buyers, and hence throw money into circulation. This is in part necessitated by the difference, if nothing else, in the periods of production, and thus of the turnovers, of the various commodity-capitals. So with this £500 II buys from I means of production of the same value and I buys from II articles of consumption valued at £500. Hence the money flows back to II.

In the case of the commodity-product I equal to 4,000c, the entire product consists of means of production, of buildings, machinery, vessels, raw and auxiliary materials, etc. So far as it goes into circulation, it circulates within class I.

Variable capital and surplus-value
in both departments

On the assumption of simple reproduction the total value of the annually produced articles of consumption is equal to the annual value-product, i.e., equal to the total value produced during the year by social labour and this must be so, because in simple reproduction this entire value is consumed.

Because IIc is equal to I$(v+s)$, then II$(c+v+s)$ is

equal to II(v+s)+ I(v+s), hence the total value of the annual product is equal to the sum of the variable capital and surplus-value. Taking our scheme. We have, after the exchange of the elements considered between I and II, and within II:

I. 4,000c + 1,000v + 1,000s (the later 2,000 realized
        in articles of consumption of IIc) = 6,000

II. 2,000c [reproduced by exchange with I(v+s)]
                            + 500v + 500s = 3,000

Sum of values = 9,000

Value newly produced during the year is contained only in v and s. The sum of the value-product of this year is therefore equal to the sum of v + s, or 2,000 I(v+s) + 1,000 II(v+s) = 3,000. All remaining value-parts of the product of this year are merely value transferred from the value of earlier means of production consumed in the annual production.

Replacement of fixed capital

Suppose the commodity-value 2,000 IIc contains 200 for replacement of wear and tear, which must be stored up in the form of money that will eventually be paid out when the fixed capital has to be replaced. The exchange would then be:

I. $1,000v + 1,000s$

II. $1,800c$ + $200c(d)$ dechet:
                            Wear and tear

Class II consists of capitalists whose fixed capital is in the most diverse stages of its reproduction. In the case of some of them it has arrived at the stage where it must be entirely replaced in kind. In the case of the others it is more or less remote from that stage. All the members of the latter group have this in common. That their fixed capital is not actually reproduced, but that its value is successively accumulated in money.

The first group is in quite the same (or almost in the same) position as when it started in business, when it came on the market with its money-capital in order to convert it into constant (fixed and circulating) capital and labour-power (variable capital). They have once more to advance this money-capital to the circulation.

The first section of II has its fixed capital-value once more in renewed bodily form, while the second section is still engaged in accumulating it in money-form for the subsequent replacement of its fixed capital in kind. It is evident that the fixed component part of constant capital II, which is reconverted into money to the full extent of its value and therefore must be renewed in kind each year (section 1), should be equal to the annual depreciation of the other fixed component part of constant capital II (section 2), which continues to function in its old bodily form and whose wear and tear, depreciation in value, which it transfers to the commodities in whose production it is engaged, is first to be compensated in money. Such a balance would seem to be a law of reproduction on the same scale. This is equivalent to saying that in class I, which puts out the means of production, the proportional division of labour must remain unchanged, since it produces on the one hand circulating and on the other fixed component parts of constant capital of department II.

If IIc (section 1) is greater than IIc (section2), foreign commodities (fixed means of production) must be imported to take up the money-surplus in I s. If, conversely, IIc (section 1) is smaller than IIc (section 2), commodities II (articles of consumption) will have to be exported to realize the depreciation part of IIc (section 2) fixed means of production. Consequently in either case foreign trade is necessary.

Accumulation and reproduction
on an extended scale

If surplus-value is being accumulated by

transforming it into additional elements of productive capital, then the amount must be sufficient under the given technical conditions either to expand the functioning constant capital or to establish a new industrial business. But it may also happen that surplus-value must be converted into money and this money hoarded for a much longer time before this process, i.e., before real accumulation, expansion of production, can take place. In order that the money (the surplus-value hoarded in money-form) may be converted into elements of productive capital, one must be able to buy these elements on the market as commodities. It makes no difference if they are not bought as finished products but made to order.

They must exist potentially, i.e., in their elements, as it requires only the impulse of an order, that is, the purchase of commodities before they actually exist and their anticipated sale, for their production really to take place. The money on the one side then calls forth extended reproduction on the other, because the possibility of it exists *without* money. For money in itself is not an element of real reproduction.

Accumulation in department I

One part of the capitalists (we call B type) is continually converting its potential money-capital, grown to an appropriate size, into productive capital, i.e., with the money hoarded by the conversion of surplus-value into money they buy means of production, additional elements of constant capital. Another part of the capitalists (we call A type) is meanwhile still engaged in hoarding its potential money-capital. The capitalists that are hoarding their surplus-value throw commodities into circulation without withdrawing other commodities in return. The capitalists converting their hoards into productive capital throw money into circulation and withdraw only commodities from it. These commodities, according to their bodily form and their destination, enter into their constant capital as fixed or circulating elements.

The sale of that portion of Is which forms the hoards of A, A', A'' is balanced by the purchase of that portion of Is which converts the hoards of B, B', B'' into elements of additional productive capital. So far as the balance is restored by the fact that the buyer acts later on as a seller to the same amount of value, and vice versa. The money returns to the side that advanced it purchasing. The balance can be maintained only on the assumption that in amount the value of the one-sided purchases and that of the one-sided sales tally. Whether it is on a simple or on an extended scale – conditions which change into so many conditions of abnormal movement into so many conditions of crises, since a balance is itself an accident owing to the spontaneous nature of this production.

In the case under consideration, the surplus-product of A, A', A'', etc. I. consists of means of production of means of production. It is only when it reaches the hands of B, B', B'', etc. I. that this surplus-product functions as additional constant capital. In order that the transition from simple to extended reproduction may take place, production in department I. must be in a position to fabricate fewer elements of constant capital for II. and so many more for I.. This transition, which does not always take place without difficulties, is facilitated by the fact that some of the products of I. may serve as means of production in either department.

Accumulation in department II

An initial scheme for accumulation on an extended scale:

I. $4,000c + 1,000v + 1,000s = 6,000$
II. $1,500c + 750v + 750s = 3,000$
                        total   9,000

The exchange of $(1,000v + 1000s)$ I, equal to $2,000$ I(v+s), for $1,500$ IIc leaves a surplus of $500s$ for accumulation in class I. But this only explains expansion of production in class I.

Now let us assume that 400 of the 500 I s are to be converted into constant capital, and 100 into variable capital. The exchange within I. of the 400s, which are thus capitalized, has already been discussed. They can therefore be annexed to Ic, and in that case we get for I...

4,400c + 1,000v + 100s (to be converted into 100v)

II. in turn buys from I. for the purpose of accumulation of the 100s (existing in means of production) which now form additional constant capital II., while the 100 in money which it pays for them are converted into the money-form of the additional variable capital of I.. We then have for I a capital of 4,400c + 1,100v (the latter in money), equalling 5,500.

II. has now 1,600c for its constant capital. In order to put them to work, it must advance a further 50v in money for the purchase of new labour-power, so that its variable capital grows from 750 to 800. This expansion of the constant and variable capital of II. by a total of 150 is supplied out of its surplus-value. Hence only 600s of the 750 IIs remain as a consumption-fund for capitalists II., whose annual product is now distributed as follows:

II. 1,600c+800v+600s(consumption-fund) = 3,000

The arrangement changed for the purpose of accumulation is now as follows:

I. 4,400c + 1,100v + 500(consumption fund) = 6,000

II. 1,600c + 800v + 600(consumption fund) = 3,000

Total, as before,   9,000

Of these amounts, the following are capital:

I.   4,400c + 1,100v (money) = 5,500
II.   1,600c +   800v (money) = 2,400
                total   7,900

While production started out with

I. $4,000c + 1,000v = 5,000$

II. $1,500c + 750v = 2,250$ total 7,250

Now, if actual accumulation takes place on this basis, that is to say, if production really goes on with this augmented capital, we obtain at the end of the following year:

I. $4,400c + 1,100v + 1,100s = 6,600$

II. $1,600c + 800v + 800s = 3,200$

total   9,800

In the exchange of I(v+s) for IIc we must meet various cases. In simple reproduction both of them must be equal and replace one another, since otherwise simple reproduction cannot proceed without disturbance, as we have seen above.

In accumulation it is above all the rate of accumulation that must be considered. In the preceding cases we assumed that the rate of accumulation in I was equal to ½s I, and also that it remained constant from year to year. We changed only the proportion in which this accumulated capital was divided into variable and constant capital.

We then had three cases:

1) I. (v+½s) equals IIc, which is therefore smaller than I. (v+s).This must always be so, otherwise I does not accumulate.

2) I. (v+½s) is greater than IIc. In this case the replacement is effected by adding a corresponding portion of IIs to IIc, so that this sum becomes equal to I (v+1/2s). Here the replacement for II is not a simple reproduction of its constant capital, but accumulation, an augmentation of its constant capital by that portion of its surplus-product which it exchanges for means of production of I.. This augmentation implies at the same time a corresponding addition to variable capital II. out of its own surplus-product.

3) I. (v+ ½s) is smaller than IIc. In this case II does not fully reproduce its constant capital by

means of exchange and must make good the deficit by purchase from I. But this does not entail any further accumulation of variable capital II, since its constant capital is fully reproduced only by this operation. On the other hand, that part of capitalists I. who accumulate only additional money-capital, have already accomplished a portion of this accumulation by this transaction.

The fact of capitalist accumulation tends to exclude the possibility of IIc being equal to I. $(v+s)$. Nevertheless it might occur even with capitalist accumulation. It might become not only equal but even bigger than I. $(v+s)$. This would mean an over-production in II. and could not be adjusted in any other way than by a great crash, in consequence of which some capital of II. would get transferred to I..

If I. s/x is taken as that portion of I. s which is spent by capitalists I. as revenue, I. $(v+s/x)$ may be equal to, larger or smaller than, II. c. But I. $(v+s/x)$ must always be smaller than II. $(c+s)$ by as much as that portion of II. s which must be consumed under all circumstances by capitalists class II.

Conclusion

Volume two describes how capital circulates through the productive processes of the economy, emerging as commodities which are transformed into money and then into materials for renewed production and so on repeatedly.

Three main categories of commodity are identified. One being *means of production*. These are buildings, machines, and raw materials etc., that are used to produce the second category, *articles of consumption*. The third category is *means of production of means of production*.

These categories can be subdivided. The categories and subdivisions are continually changing as are their proportions, in order to meet market requirements. However, in order for the economy to function the categories must be produced in definite proportions to each other. In a free market these proportions are maintained by supply and demand. In large organisations there will be planning, but externally the organisation will operate in a free market environment. Following is an example of an economy that balances and where the 100% surplus-value is consumed by the capitalist class and fixed capital is ignored.

I.   Production of Means of Production:

Capital

$$4,000c + 1,000v = 5,000$$

Commodity-Product

$$4,000c + 1,000v + 1,000s = 6,000 \text{ in means of production.}$$

II   Production of Articles of Consumption

Capital

$$2,000c + 500v = 2,500$$

68

Commodity-Product

2,000c + 500v + 500s = 3,000 in articles of
consumption

c   indicates constant capital (raw materials and machinery etc.)

v   indicates variable capital (labour-power)

s   indicates surplus-value (labour expended in excess of that required to produce the labour's subsistence)

In order for the economy to balance the following equalities must be achieved.

I.4,000c+   II. 2,000c   =   6,000
(total means of production)

I.1,000v + I.1,000s + II.500v + II.500s = 3,000
(total of articles of consumption)

$$I.1,000v + I.1,000s = II.2,000c$$

(consumption by section I.) = (means of production used in section II.)

Imbalances should have a tendency to correct themselves by market forces, but unusual factors can severely disrupt the market. Such as a crisis caused by over production. Recovery usually starts at the bottom, but if interference comes from the top and ignores the market then conditions can get worse. Failing institutions should be allowed to fail, that is how capitalism works. The "*too big to fail*" is simply declaring the divine right of bankers.

A little book about butterflies

GW01080058

National Museum Wales Books

First published in 2008 by National
Museum Wales Books, Cathays
Park, Cardiff, CF10 3NP, Wales.

© National Museum of Wales

ISBN 978-0-7200-0596-7

Text: Siân Davies, David Jenkins,
Robert Protheroe-Jones
Design: Peter Gill & Associates
Editing and production: Mari Gordon
Also available in Welsh as
Llyfr bach am beiriannau mawr,
ISBN 978-0-7200-0597-4

Sponsored by
Welsh Assembly
Government

Contents

Foreword

After its great natural beauty, Wales is perhaps best known as an industrial nation. Indeed, many claim that Wales was the world's first industrial nation, where more people worked in industry than agriculture. Certainly over the past three centuries the country has played host to many world-class inventions and innovations in mining, metal manufacture and transport.

The National Waterfront Museum in Swansea celebrates this in an exciting and dynamic way. It puts people and communities at the heart of the story of Welsh industrialisation, and provides an inspiring venue to display some of the key objects that help tell that tale.

Among the many thousands of objects in the Museum, a number impress not only with their historical importance but also with their sheer size. Some were firsts for Wales and in the world, others were more common but still fundamental to the dynamism of Welsh industry.

This is a little book that celebrates the 'big things' that have contributed so much to the industrial history of our nation.

Steph Mastoris
Head of the National Waterfront Museum

Richard Trevithick's steam locomotive

In 1803, the Merthyr ironmaster Samuel Homfray brought Richard Trevithick to his Penydarren ironworks. Homfray was interested in the high pressure engines that the Cornishman had developed and installed in his road engines, and he encouraged Trevithick to look into the possibility of converting such an engine into a rail-mounted locomotive to travel over the newly laid tramroad from Penydarren to the canal wharf at Abercynon. It would appear that Trevithick started work on the locomotive in the autumn of 1803 and, by February 1804, it was completed. Tradition has it that Richard Crawshay, owner of the nearby Cyfarthfa ironworks, was highly sceptical about the new engine, and he and Homfray placed a wager of 500 guineas each with Richard Hill (of the Plymouth ironworks) as to whether or not the engine could haul ten tons of iron to Abercynon, and haul the empty wagons back.

The first run was on 21 February, and was described in some detail by Trevithick:

"…yesterday we proceeded on our journey with the engine, and we carried ten tons of iron in five wagons, and seventy men riding on them the whole of the journey …the engine, while working, went nearly five miles an hour; there was no water put into the boiler from the time we started until our journey's end …the coal consumed was two hundredweight".

Unfortunately, on the return journey a bolt sheared, causing the boiler to leak. The fire then had to be dropped and the engine did not get back to Penydarren until the following day. This gave Crawshay reason to claim that the run had not been completed as stipulated in the wager, but it is not known if this was ever settled! The engine was, in fact, too heavy for the rails. Later, it would serve as a stationary engine driving a forge hammer at the Penydarren works.

Left: Terence Cuneo's spirited portrayal of Richard Trevithick supervising the inaugural run of the locomotive on 21 February 1804.

Below: In December 1989, the BBC was filming a documentary series entitled *The Birth of Europe*. The programme dealt with the industrialization of Europe and was based in part around the replica locomotive. The loco's regular driver, the late Dave Lloyd, donned period costume to re-create this splendid, brooding portrait of Trevithick.

Right: The locomotive in steam at the Welsh Industrial & Maritime Museum in 1983.

The replica locomotive on display in the Museum today was planned in the late 1970s, working from Trevithick's documents and plans, now in the National Museum of Science and Industry. Built in the workshop of the Welsh Industrial & Maritime Museum in Cardiff, it incorporated components sourced from a wide range of engineering companies operating in south Wales at that time. It was inaugurated in 1981 and, ironically, presented the exact same problem as the original engine – it too broke the rails on which it ran! Before coming to the National Waterfront Museum, it was on display at the National Railway Museum in York, and had a starring role in Railfest 200, a celebration of the bicentenary of the original engine's pioneering run.

We cannot underestimate the importance of Trevithick's locomotive. In 1800, the fastest a man could travel over land was at a gallop on horseback; a century later, much of the world had an extensive railway system on which trains regularly travelled at speeds of up to sixty miles per hour. This remarkable transformation, a momentous occasion in world history, was initiated in south Wales in that February of 1804.

Right: The replica locomotive in its present home, the National Waterfront Museum.

Left: The replica locomotive and
its attendant bar iron 'bogies' at its
former home, the Welsh Industrial
& Maritime Museum, in 1983.

13

The coal wagon

Coal wagons like this one first began to appear on the developing UK rail network in the mid-nineteenth century. Their origins can be traced to the horse-drawn 'chaldron' wagons used on colliery tramways in the north-east of England. By the early 1850s, there were a few thousand smaller, seven-ton wagons in use in south Wales. However, by the 1880s, wagons similar to this one, capable of loading ten tons of coal, were becoming the standard on British railways. This example is built to a later design agreed by the Railway Clearing House in 1923, and came from Cwm Colliery near Llantrisant.

One side of the wagon is painted in the bold livery of the Ocean Coal Company. This was the company founded by David Davies of Llandinam – 'Davies the Ocean' – and in its heyday it was one of the foremost producers of steam coal in south Wales. The monolithic status of this large enterprise is reflected in the simple, bold livery; the term 'OCEAN' reflects the widespread use of the company's coal in the stokeholds of steamships all over the globe. The other side of the wagon is painted in the livery of the Cwmgwrach colliery in the upper Neath valley, a colliery that produced anthracite coal. As was often the case with anthracite colliery wagons, the livery takes the form of a mobile advertisement, describing the many uses – lime burning, malting or hop-drying – for anthracite, which burnt with intense heat and gave off no sulphurous fumes.

Left: The coal wagon on display at the National Waterfront Museum.

At the height of the coal trade in 1913, there were about 100,000 private wagons in use in south Wales. They were owned by builders such as the Cambrian Wagon Works in Cardiff, who leased them to the collieries. The leasing companies kept an individual record card for each wagon, and the wagon was periodically recalled for repairs or a complete overhaul.

At that time an enormous number of coal trains also ran on the railways of south Wales. In 1900, about 100 coal trains of some fifty wagons and a brake van passed through Pontypridd on weekdays, being either 'down' coal trains or 'up' empties. Because there was so little room in the narrow mining valleys to lay out sidings, it was essential that deliveries of empty wagons to collieries, and their prompt collection after loading, progressed as smoothly as possible or terrible disruption could result.

At the ports, where there was plenty of flat land, marshalling yards were laid out to organize the trains for tipping into ships' holds. As the wagons only had doors for tipping at one end, they had to be marshalled so that they faced the right way round on the tracks. Moreover, if the order specified a mixture of coals, two different trains had to be marshalled on adjacent tracks to tip wagons of different grades of coal into the ship's hold.

CWMGWRACH

BIG VEIN ANTHRACITE

LARGE, COBBLES &

FOR MALTING, HOP DRYING

CAERBRYN & EMPIRE COLLIERIES

Nº 426

For Repairs Advise
The North Central Wagon Cº Lᵈ
Cardiff
Load 10 Tons

After the nationalisation of the railways, steel-bodied successors to the wooden wagons were built in large numbers, and they continued to be used for coal traffic in south Wales until the mid-1980s. The few coal trains still operating in the area today are made up of large hopper wagons, which discharge their load through opening bottoms.

Left: A coal wagon is tipped into a steamer's hold at Barry Docks, around 1905.

Above: Rakes of wagons containing different types of coal can be seen on the sidings leading to this tip at the North Dock, Newport, in March 1927. Depending on the order, it was common practice to tip alternate wagons of different grades and sizes of coal into a ship's holds to obtain the mixture specified by the customer.

Right: This is thought to be Ystrad Station on the Taff Vale Railway in the Rhondda Fawr, in the 1880s. An 'up' train of empty Ocean Coal Company wagons travels up the valley, passing a 'down' train of loaded wagons heading for Cardiff or Penarth Docks.

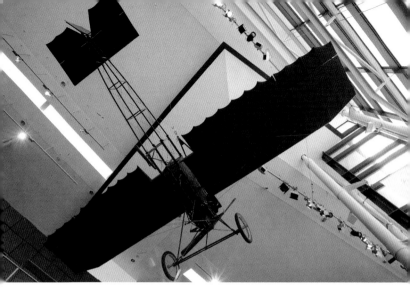

The *Robin Goch* monoplane

The *Robin Goch* (Welsh for 'robin redbreast') plane is one of the few amateur aeroplanes built before 1914 to survive. It's the only field plane of its kind in Wales, and one of the earliest examples of aircraft in the United Kingdom.

The plane was built by Charles Horace Watkins around 1908 at a cost of £300 at Mynachdy Farm in Maindy, Cardiff. Watkins reputedly started to design and build the three cylinder 40hp engine in 1907. The propeller is date-stamped 1908, but was apparently abandoned early on due to poor performance; the two replacement propellers have not survived.

The plane is 6,554mm long, its wingspan is 9,754mm and its overall height is 2,439mm; its empty weight is 250.84 kg. The fuselage of the plane is an open wooden structure, cross-braced with piano wire and with the cockpit partially enclosed. The pilot's seat came from a kitchen chair. Apart from moving the tailplane to the top of the fuselage, the rudder and tailplane are unaltered from the original structure.

The undercarriage was originally made of oak but was immediately replaced by a tubular steel structure. Inside the cockpit there is a level for longitudinal reading, a ball-in-cage for lateral indication, a clock and three-minute egg timer for speed and navigation calculations, and a voltmeter. For night-time flying the instruments were illuminated by lights.

We know that Watkins discussed the topic of flight with the Cardiff airship pioneer, Ernest Williams. Watkins also met the pioneer British aviator Gustav Hamel when he came to Cardiff to give a public flying display in 1914. Local newspapers from that day reported that Hamel went to see the *Robin Goch* with Watkins.

Watkins said that he had flown the monoplane on several occasions in and around Cardiff sometime before 1914. There are no known reports or evidence to support this claim, however, the *Robin Goch* was examined by engineers at RAF St Athan in the 1960s and they concluded that it was certainly airworthy.

Left: The *Robin Goch* suspended high above visitors' heads at the National Waterfront Museum.

Left: Charles Watkins standing next to the *Robin Goch's* propeller, about 1910.

Above: Charles Watkins (left) with the pioneering aviator Gustav Hamel (centre) during his visit to Cardiff on 28 March 1914.

After the port cylinder-head fractured in 1916, it did not fly again. Watkins dismantled his plane and kept the pieces in a good state of repair in his garage in Colum Road in Cardiff. In 1961, a neighbour who worked for the RAF became intrigued and persuaded Watkins to supervise the re-assembly of the plane at St Athan, where it was displayed with other historic aircraft before being donated to the Museum in 1995.

Charles Horace Watkins died in 1976, aged 91. He can not only claim to be an innovative engineer, but also to being the first man to design and construct an aeroplane in Wales.

Above: The tailplane shows the plane's name, and the initials of its builder.

The tilt hammer

From earliest times, the most important ironworking tool was the hammer. Hammers were used by forgemen, to manufacture wrought iron bars, and smiths, who used those bars to make products ranging from chains and horseshoes to armour and weapons. However, the power of the human arm is limited. When water wheels began to be widely used to power machinery in medieval times, the iron industry was one of the first to use this new technology, initially to power large hammers.

Different varieties of water-powered hammers evolved for the different branches of the iron industry. Slower, heavier-hitting ones were used in forges, and lighter, fast-hitting ones used by smiths. This reflected the type of work they undertook: forgemen worked on thicker iron that needed heavier blows, smiths worked on thinner iron that cooled fast and needed rapid, lighter blows.

During the nineteenth century steam and, later, compressed air superseded water power for iron forging and smithing. However, a few water-powered hammers survived into the twentieth century, mainly in rural areas. They survived longest in the specialised trade of tool manufacture – notably shovels and edge tools such as sickles and billhooks. A few water-powered forges survived – usually disused – until the 1950s and 1960s when their historic importance was appreciated, resulting in their preservation on-site or in museums.

Right: The tilt hammer, made from a wych elm beam and hand-forged ironwork, on display at the National Waterfront Museum.

Wales was a major centre of the British iron industry from the late seventeenth century. The industry originated due to the widespread availability of iron ore, wood for making charcoal to fuel the processes and fast-flowing rivers to power machinery. In the early nineteenth century the Welsh iron industry was internationally pre-eminent and pioneered many innovations.

The last water-powered forge to work in Wales was a shovel forge at Aberaeron in Ceredigion, where the Museum's tilt hammer was installed in 1850. The forge replaced an earlier one a few miles away, and the hammer probably incorporates parts of a hammer from the older sickle forge established in 1800. The water wheel drove the hammer at a speed of 140 blows a minute. Wrought iron (or later steel) bars were bought-in, cut to length,

heated up and forged into shovels and sickles. The forgeman sat in front of the hammer on a seat suspended from the rafters – this enabled him to change the position of the work in relation to the hammer. He held the work in a pair of blacksmith's tongs. Other tools such as spades, scythes and forks were probably also manufactured. In the early twentieth century the main product of the forge was pointed, long-handled shovels, typically used both in agriculture

Left: The hammer's 'tappet wheel', which was driven by a water wheel and whose teeth activated the hammer.

Above: The hammer's massive cast iron head.

and in the mid-Wales lead mines. Shovels of this shape were known in the area as *rhaw Aberaeron* ('Aberaeron shovel'). The forge operated until the early 1940s, and the tilt hammer was donated to the Museum in 1959.

Above: The forging stages of a shovel, from a billet of steel to the finished shovel.

Right: The forgeman manipulating the steel beneath the hammer; an assistant controlled the supply of water to the waterwheel.

The tinplate rolling mill

Much of the produce of the modern steel industry is sheets used for cars, domestic appliances and roofing. Sheets are also cut up and formed into all manner of small components. The technology needed to produce sheet steel can be traced directly back to the development of the world's first rolling mill for wide sheet iron in 1697. It was developed in Pontypool, by the workmen of John Hanbury. Good quality sheet iron was a vital part of tinplate manufacture, and by the 1720s Hanbury had perfected tinplate manufacture, an industry that Wales dominated for almost two hundred years.

Tinplate was initially used for kitchenwares. By the late nineteenth century canned foods were very important, enabling the transport of foods around the world and the storage of seasonal fruits and vegetables. Major food industries such as Argentinean corned beef and Alaskan salmon all relied on Welsh tinplate.

Before the development of tankers, the petroleum industry used cans made from sheets that were coated with a cheaper mixture of lead and tin. These too were mostly Welsh-made. By the early 1890s eighty per cent of the world's tinplate was produced in Wales.

Until automation in the mid-twentieth century, the tinplate industry was labour intensive. At its peak in the 1920s it employed over 30,000 Welsh men and women.

Right: The end of one of the mill's rolls. Millbrook Foundry, in Swansea, was one of a number of Welsh foundries that specialised in casting rolls.

Bars of iron (or, from around 1880, steel) were heated and rolled into thin sheets. These were then heated and carefully cooled ('annealed') to soften them, then cleaned in acid. The sheets were then cold-rolled, annealed again and cleaned in acid again before being dipped in molten tin. The very thin tin coating was polished, the sheets were graded by quality, then boxed-up for despatch around the world.

The initial hot rolling was key to the quality of the tinned sheets. Because thin sheets cool very quickly, they were repeatedly folded in half to conserve heat (and to keep the lengthening sheets from becoming unmanageable). Eventually they formed a 'pack' eight sheets thick. Swiftness was also essential – the rollerman entered them into the rolls and the 'behinder' passed them back over the upper roll for further rolling.

At intervals they were slid across the floor to the 'doubler' to fold them in half. When the sheets cooled they were again slid across the floor to the furnaceman who placed them in the coal-fired furnace to reheat them, and slid newly heated sheets back to the rollerman. The crew used long tongs to handle the sheets, as they were about 800°C.

Left: The 'rollerman' entering a sheet into the rolls at Clayton Works in Pontardulais in 1957.

Above: The 'behinder' returning a pair of singles to the 'rollerman'.

Over the course of a shift, each man handled the equivalent of fifty tons of metal. An observer described it as 'an industrial ballet of precise teamwork'.

The Museum's rolling mill operated from 1911 to 1957 at Melingriffith Tinplate Works in Cardiff. In 1911, over 500 mills of this type were working in tinplate works in Wales, and around 100 in galvanised sheet works. The mill was cast at South Wales Foundry in Llanelli, and the rolls at Millbrook Foundry in Swansea. It was donated to the Museum in 1958.

Above: Handling a hot sheet at Clayton Works, Pontardulais in 1957.

RICHARD THOMAS & Co Ld
STEEL
1910
LLANELLY

Left: South Wales Foundry in Llanelli was owned by Richard Thomas & Co Ltd, and was one of only three specialist foundries in Wales equipped to produce large steel castings.

Above: The rolls, up close.

The brick press

Although Wales is usually thought of as a land of stone-built buildings, bricks have been widely made, especially from the clay, marls and shales of south and north-east Wales, and from the fireclays that underlie coal seams.

The wide variety of raw materials made bricks of very different qualities and colours. Marls, shales and clays usually made red bricks, but some were orange or even purple. Depending on their quality, they were used for general building, engineering work or paving. Fireclays, a by-product of coal mining, made yellow or even white bricks. Most were used in furnaces, thanks to their heat resisting properties, but some were suitable for general building work.

In some places very pure silica sandstones were quarried and processed into bricks suitable for high temperature furnaces. This industry originated at Craig y Ddinas at the head of the Vale of Neath. Such was the reputation of these bricks that, until the 1960s, the word for 'silica brick' in French, German and Russian was 'Dinas'.

Floor tiles, roof tiles and drainage pipes were made in some works – the red 'quarry tiles' made in the Ruabon district are well known.

Left: Bricks emerging from the press on display at the National Waterfront Museum.

In the third quarter of the nineteenth century machinery came into general use to finely mill the raw materials and to mould and press the bricks. These machine-made bricks were more consistent and of higher quality than hand-made bricks. Most of the machinery used throughout the twentieth century could trace its arrangement to mid-nineteenth century innovations. The brick press displayed in the Museum is a late nineteenth-century design that derives from a machine patented in 1859. It comes from Emlyn Colliery Brickworks, Penygroes, Carmarthenshire. The works operated from the 1890s until 2000, processing waste shale and, in the 1990s, clay from opencast coal sites. Many Welsh collieries had brickworks that used clay and waste shale as raw materials and burnt the bricks using unsaleable small coal.

Analysis of the layers of paint on the press indicated that it had been assembled from parts of a number

of different presses. It appears to be a factory reconditioned press made in the 1960s from second-hand parts by Fawcett-Craven of Leeds, successors to Bradley & Craven Ltd, the original manufacturers.

The press consists of three main parts. A vertical 'worm' forced ground clay into one of sixteen moulds in a revolving circular 'clot table'. As the table revolved, the 'clots' (part-formed bricks) were ejected and pushed into the press unit at the front of the press. In this, a vertical press forced each clot into a mould and stamped a depression ('frog') and the name of the works into each finished brick. The bricks were then fired in a coal-fuelled kiln for up to a week. The press produced 10,000 bricks a day.